ExpLosions

Becca Heddle

OXFORD

UNIVERSITY PRESS

OXFORD
UNIVERSITY PRESS

Great Clarendon Street, Oxford OX2 6DP

Oxford University Press is a department of the University of Oxford.
It furthers the University's objective of excellence in research, scholarship,
and education by publishing worldwide in

Oxford   New York

Auckland   Cape Town   Dar es Salaam   Hong Kong   Karachi
Kuala Lumpur   Madrid   Melbourne   Mexico City   Nairobi
New Delhi   Shanghai   Taipei   Toronto

With offices in

Argentina   Austria   Brazil   Chile   Czech Republic   France   Greece
Guatemala   Hungary   Italy   Japan   Poland   Portugal   Singapore
South Korea   Switzerland   Thailand   Turkey   Ukraine   Vietnam

Oxford is a registered trade mark of Oxford University Press
in the UK and in certain other countries

British Library Cataloguing in Publication Data

Data available

ISBN 978-0-19-917946-6

21

Printed in China by Golden Cup

Acknowledgements

The publisher would like to thank the following for permission to reproduce
photographs: **p4** Corbis/Stocktrek, **p5** Corbis/Rosenthal Zade/Sygma, **p8**t Alamy/FLPA, b Alamy/Robert
Harding Picture Library, **p10** The Perfect Image/Photographers Direct, **p11**t Alamy/Brand X Pictures, r
Corbis/Kevin R Morris, **p12 & 13** Kimbolton Fireworks, **p15** Corbis/Alan Schein Photography, **p16** Science
Photo Library, **p17**t Corbis/Bettmann, b Corbis/Hulton Archive, **p18 & 19** www.implosion-world.com
(http://www.implosion-world.com), **p21** Corbis/Cooperphoto, **p23**b Alamy/FLPA, t Corbis, **p24** US Geological
Survey, **p25**t Alamy/Dennis Hallinan, c Corbis/Gary Braasch, b Alamy, Robert Harding Picture Library, **p27**t
Corbis, b Corbis/Bettmann, **p28**l Corbis/Joseph Sohm;Visions of America, b Corbis/Reuters, **p29**t Science Photo
Library/Hank Morgan, b Greenpeace, **p30**t Lee Marquis Photography/Photographers Direct, b Corbis/RF

Cover photography by: Getty/Akira Kaede

Illustrations by: **p5**, **p7**, **p9**, **p15**, **p19**, **p20**b, **p22**, **p26** Matt Buckley, **p6**b, **p16**, **p21**
Martin Cottam, **p10/11** Mark Duffin, **p6**t, **p14**, **p20**t Gary Swift

Design by Chrome-Dome Design

Every effort has been made to contact copyright holders of material reproduced in this book. If notified,
the publishers will be pleased to rectify any errors or omissions at the earliest opportunity

CONTENTS

Crash, bang, wallop   4

Fireworks through time   6

Fireworks directory   8

Fireworks around the world   10

Setting up a display   12

Too dangerous?   14

Don't blow it up!   15

Blowing up buildings   16

How to demolish a building   18

Blowing up food   20

Nature's explosions   22

A mountain explodes   24

Nuclear explosions   26

The Chernobyl accident   28

Bang!   30

Glossary   31

Index   32

CRASH BANG WALLOP

Explosions are amazing, terrifying and sometimes exciting, all at the same time. But how do they happen, and how many different types are there? This book is about all sorts of explosions.

Fireworks are probably the kind of explosion we are most familiar with and like the best. Nuclear bombs are probably the most destructive and terrifying. But there are all sorts of other explosions, from huge volcanoes to the pops of popcorn and Christmas crackers.

Many of the different sorts of explosions are dangerous. When something explodes, it expands very quickly, to release a build-up of pressure. If the pressure is blocked by something, it will push whatever that is out of the way, possibly breaking it into tiny pieces which will fly out with great force.

For example, if you heat baby food in a jar, the food gets hot and makes steam. If you leave the lid on tightly, pressure builds up inside because the steam can't escape. If the jar explodes, glass and hot food fly in all directions and can cut and burn anyone standing in the way.

Some kinds of explosions carry added dangers – often from the effects of extreme heat, like in a gas explosion, or **radioactivity** in a nuclear one. But there is still no doubt that we find the sudden bangs and flashes, as can be seen in this film stunt, exciting and enticing, as well as frightening.

FIREWORKS THROUGH TIME

The first place anyone recorded seeing fireworks was in China. It all started in the 500s, when the first firecrackers were exploded. They were just lengths of bamboo thrown onto fires – but as they heated up, the gases inside them expanded and the canes exploded with an enormous bang. Later, the explorer **Marco Polo** described how horses were tied up with their eyes and ears covered, to stop them from being frightened by this noise.

Proper fireworks began with the invention of gunpowder. Again, they started in China, and a whole range of fireworks was made – including rockets, sparklers and coloured flames. Western writers in the 1220s described these fireworks and started writing down 'recipes' of how to make them.

The simplest fireworks are rockets: each rocket is a tube with gunpowder packed inside it. There is a **fuse** into the gunpowder and a small hole in the bottom of the tube. When the fuse is lit, the powder burns. The gases made by the burning powder shoot out of the hole in the bottom and push the rocket up into the sky.

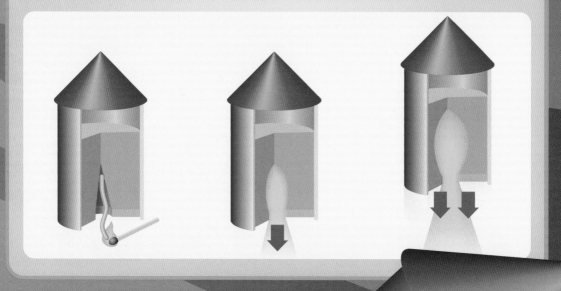

Display rockets have a second fuse which leads to more gunpowder and small fireworks, such as sparklers, coloured lights, crackers or star shells. The second fuse sets off this gunpowder when the rocket is high in the sky, to explode and spread the other fireworks around.

FIREWORKS DIRECTORY

CATHERINE WHEEL

As its name suggests, this is shaped like a wheel and can turn around. It is set off nailed to a post. The charges are set up so that when they burn they make the wheel turn round. Chemicals in the different parts make different colours.

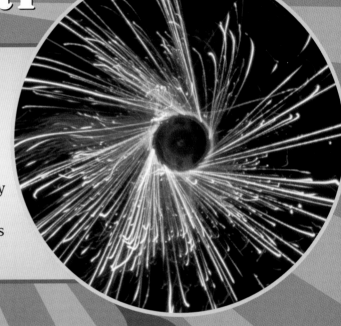

SPARKLER

This is the firework you are most likely to have held. It is made of a length of wire, with a mixture like gunpowder spread along it. It is a slightly different mixture so that it doesn't explode – it crackles and sparkles instead.

Always wear gloves when handling sparklers and keep them away from your face. Put them in a bucket of earth or sand when they are done.

FIREWORKS IN THE AIR

There are lots of different shapes that fireworks can make in the air. If you go to a big fireworks display, see which of these you can spot:

Palm: makes a shape like a palm tree

Round shell: makes a ball shape

Ring shell: makes a ring of stars

Willow: has long-lasting stars which make a pattern like willow branches – you might even still be able to see them when they land on the ground

Roundel: draws a circle in the sky

Maroon: makes a loud bang

Chrysanthemum: makes a big ball shape of stars that leave a trail as they fall

Serpentine: sends little tubes outwards in squiggly paths – they may explode into stars at the end of their journey

FIREWORKS AROUND THE WORLD

Fireworks are set off during celebrations all around the world. Sometimes they mark international festivals, like New Year, or religious ones, like Easter. Sometimes they are for weddings or big parties. What is clear is that people love having an excuse to fill the sky with light and sound. Here is a selection of some of the occasions when fireworks are set off in different countries.

Dublin, Ireland: St Patrick's Day celebrations on 17 March

Scotland: Hogmanay (New Year) celebrations

USA: 4 July, Independence Day

Mexico: at Easter, models of **Judas** filled with fireworks are exploded. Other models are often made too, of unpopular political figures and 'causes of evil'

England: 5 November, the anniversary of the failed **Gunpowder Plot** (Australia and New Zealand celebrate this too)

France: Bastille Day, 14 July, marks the anniversary of the beginning of the French Revolution in 1789

China: Chinese New Year, in January or February

India: Diwali, the Hindu festival of lights, in the winter months

To mark the beginning of the new millennium, on 1 January 2000, many countries set off fireworks at exactly midnight, local time. If you could have watched it from space, you would have seen fireworks set off in a tide right around the world. Since then, many countries that did not previously celebrate New Year with fireworks have turned it into an annual event.

SETTING UP A
DISPLAY

Have you ever wondered what goes into setting up a big fireworks display? Here are the details from Simon Page of Kimbolton Fireworks in the United Kingdom.

"We usually get booked about six months to a year ahead. First we visit the site. Is it in a city centre, with not much space for the fireworks to land? Are there thatched roofs or car parks nearby? We need to know, to keep the risk of fires to a minimum – then we can plan the display."

"It takes three to four weeks to get the fireworks ready, all packed together with their fuses ready for firing. Once they are ready, and no more than a fortnight before the display, we prepare the site."

"Firstly, we lay out the tubes for firing big fireworks, then lay the main cable to control the firing, and lastly we connect in all the fireworks. This can take twenty people up to ten days to do!"

KIMBOLTON
FIREWORKS

"At last we can fire the display – twenty minutes of glory."

"We set off many displays every year, but it's always a thrill. It's the best job in the world!"

"After the display, we collect any fireworks that we didn't use or that did not go off. Then we can pack everything up and take it away."

DUBLIN SKYFEST, ST PATRICK'S DAY 2005

Facts and figures

* 20km of wires
* 8,000 fireworks
* 38 different firing points
* a 20 minute display

TOO DANGEROUS?

Some people think that fireworks should be banned because every year people are hurt by them. However, it is usually because someone has broken the safety rules. Here they are.

The fireworks code

* Only buy fireworks that are marked BS7114. This means they are safety approved.

* Only people over 16 can buy fireworks.

* Keep the fireworks in a closed box, away from where you are setting them off – otherwise, sparks from other fireworks could set them off.

* Follow the instructions on each firework.

* Light all fireworks at arm's length and then stand well back.

* Never go back to a lit firework.

* Never put fireworks in your pocket.

* Never throw fireworks.

* Keep pets indoors. Fireworks frighten them and they could get hurt or even killed.

DON'T BLOW IT UP!

It is always important to think about your own safety where there is any risk of an explosion. Explosions in the home are very rare indeed, but would you know what to do if you smelt gas when you came home?

⚠ Find the gas meter and turn off the supply.

⚠ Open doors and windows to let the gas out.

⚠ Leave the house, and call the gas emergency service – their number is in the phone book, under 'Gas'.

While you're still in the building, no one must:

⚠ smoke

⚠ use the phone – not even a mobile

⚠ touch any electric switches.

If there is a gas leak, the smallest spark from a switch or phone could set off an explosion.

BLOWING UP BUILDINGS

Almost as long as people have been making buildings, they have been knocking them down, to clear space or make way for other buildings. Very small buildings can be taken apart stone by stone, and you can knock down medium-sized ones with a crane or wrecking ball – but buildings have got bigger, stronger and closer together, and that's where explosives come in.

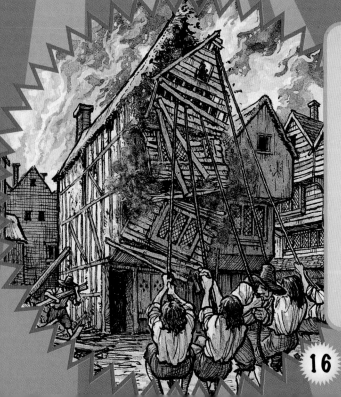

In America in the 1850s, explosives were first used to demolish unsafe buildings and to control fires. People had known for a long time that pulling down buildings in the path of a fire can stop it in its tracks, by taking away its fuel – it was one of the ways the Great Fire of London was controlled in 1666. But now that people had explosives, they could do the job much more quickly.

In 1906, San Francisco was struck by an enormous earthquake, which caused a terrible fire. By then, blowing up buildings to limit a fire's spread was completely normal. The mayor could send telegrams to surrounding communities, asking simply: "Send fire engines and dynamite, immediately." Although it took four days to put out the fires, people think the blasts saved quite a large area of the western part of the city.

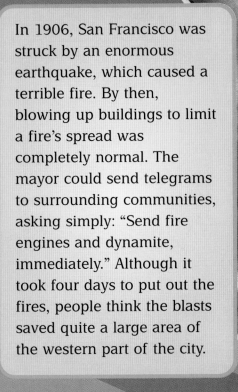

After the Second World War (1939–1945), many unsafe, bomb-damaged buildings in Europe had to be demolished and new properties built. This gave demolition experts lots of practice – and by the late 1940s, newsreels showed buildings being brought down without damaging the ones around them.

HOW TO DEMOLISH A BUILDING

If a big building needs to be demolished in the middle of a city, the best way to bring it down is to 'implode' it. This means that the building collapses in on itself, all the rubble falls in a heap exactly where the building itself stood, and the buildings around the demolished one are not damaged. But how do they make this happen?

Columns are fully loaded with explosives and hooked up to blasting caps and fuses.

First of all, the demolition experts look at the original architects' drawings of the building to see how it is put together. Then they tour the building to see it for real and decide what explosives to use and where to place them.

They set explosives at different levels in the building, drilling holes in concrete pillars to hold them and wrapping them carefully to contain the blast. Like cutting on one side of a tree to make it fall that way, they place the explosives carefully so all the pillars will fall inwards.

If you blow up the bottom of a building, **gravity** will do most of the rest of the work for you – the weight of the building landing on the bottom storeys will crush them to rubble. But the top storeys have nothing landing on them, so they need extra blasts, a little after the blasts at the bottom, to break them up too.

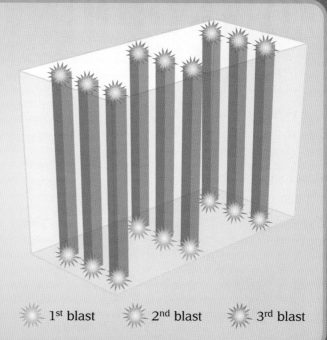

☀ 1st blast   ☀ 2nd blast   ☀ 3rd blast

Holly Bennett is the only female explosives engineer in Europe. She loves blowing up buildings.

BLOWING UP FOOD

Sometimes explosions happen in kitchens by accident – for example, if you leave a tight lid on something in a microwave. But there is one food that explodes on purpose – popcorn.

Popcorn starts off looking like dried corn on the cob, until you pop it. Then it turns right inside out and shoots into the air – it can jump up to a metre when it pops, so be careful if you are making popcorn in a pan.

hard shell

soft starch

water

Each **kernel** of corn is made of up three layers. Outside is the kernel's hard shell, then a layer of soft starch. Right in the middle is the secret explosive ingredient – water.

When you heat popcorn, the water turns into steam. Steam takes up more room than water, so pressure builds up inside the kernel. When the outer shell can't take any more pressure, the kernel just explodes. The corn turns completely inside out, so the soft bits are outside and the steam escapes.

HOW IS POPCORN DIFFERENT?

The outer shell of popcorn is harder than any other corn shell, so a lot of pressure can build up inside it before it gives way. That is what makes the pop.

If you think of popcorn as an American food, you're right – people in America have been eating popcorn for at least 4000 years. The **Aztecs** used it in ceremonies, and Native Americans both ate it and used it for decoration.

21

NATURE'S EXPLOSIONS

Did you know that when a volcano erupts, this is an explosion from the Earth itself?

The Earth has a very thin outside covering which is organised into plates. Even though the plates are massive, they can move around on the Earth's surface, pulling apart or moving underneath each other where they meet.

Just underneath some of the plates there are pockets of magma – rock that is so hot it has melted. When the plates move, the magma can move out through cracks to the surface. The places where magma leaks out become volcanoes. Some of them are on land, some are under the sea, and some build up under the sea and break the surface to become islands.

So what actually happens when a volcano erupts?

Where the Earth's crust is thin, the magma can push up through the crust. The magma's own heat can melt the rock it is pushing through, which not only makes it easier to move, it also increases the amount of magma on the move. If the pressure gets high enough, or there is a crack in the surface for it to get through, the **molten rock** can explode out onto the Earth's surface.

The island of Surtsey, off Iceland, was formed in November 1963 as the result of an underwater eruption.

There can be a long time between volcanic eruptions – sometimes so long that people think of the volcanoes as ordinary mountains. But **dormant** volcanoes can erupt and catch people out.

The next two pages tell the story of one of the biggest volcanic eruptions in recent history.

A MOUNTAIN EXPLODES

Mount St Helens is in the state of Washington in the United States of America. It had been dormant for 123 years before it erupted in May, 1980.

There had been some small earthquakes over the previous two months, and one side of the mountain had grown a suspicious bulge. Just after half past eight in the morning, this bulge exploded and the whole side of the mountain collapsed.

The explosion was so huge it was heard in Vancouver, Canada, 320 kilometres away.

A huge cloud of ash poured out of the top of the volcano as the avalanche of rock rushed down the destroyed side. The ash and gases from inside the volcano created pyroclastic flows – terrifying cascades of hot gas and ash that move at up to 500 kilometres per hour, burning everything in their path. Whole forests were destroyed.

The mountain carried on exploding for nine hours, throwing out millions of tons of ash. It took an hour and a quarter for the ash cloud to reach the city of Yakima, 145 kilometres away. It blocked out the light all day and left drifts of ash up to thirteen centimetres deep, which it took ten days to clear away.

Before the eruption: the mountain was a peaceful place, popular with tourists.

During the eruption: huge clouds of smoke, ash and chunks of rock flew out in all directions. The eruption killed 57 people.

After the eruption: the mountain was a different shape, and the forests around it would take years to recover.

NUCLEAR EXPLOSIONS

Probably the most powerful explosions we can make on Earth are the result of nuclear reactions.

HOW A NUCLEAR REACTION WORKS

Everything is made up of **atoms**, and right in the middle of the atom is the part called the nucleus. The nucleus contains particles called protons and neutrons.

In a nuclear reaction, extra neutrons are fired at atoms. When a neutron hits an atom, it blasts into the nucleus. This makes the nucleus really unstable and it blows apart, releasing more neutrons.

These neutrons then hit other atoms, and the process happens again and again, until all the fuel is used up – that is, until all the atoms have exploded. The millions of tiny explosions create a huge amount of energy.

The atom is hit by a loose neutron.

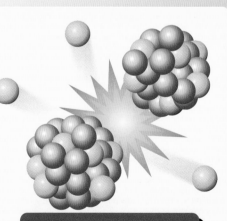

The atom explodes into smaller atoms and it releases more neutrons.

In a nuclear power station, the nuclear reactions are carefully controlled, in order to harness the energy which is made. The explosion of a nuclear bomb, however, is due to a runaway process of nuclear reactions, and so nuclear bombs are the most devastating weapons known to humankind. The temperature at the centre of the blast can be up to 300 million degrees Celsius.

The only nuclear bombs ever to be used against people destroyed the Japanese cities of Hiroshima and Nagasaki, on August 6 and 9, 1945. They killed over 200,000 people, and the radioactivity left behind has affected the lives of millions more.

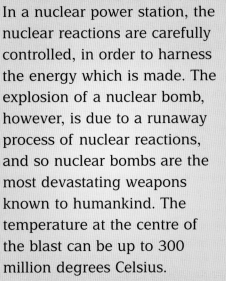

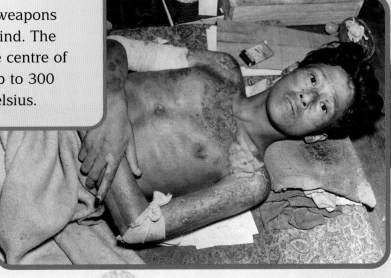

THE CHERNOBYL ACCIDENT

Nuclear power plants create a great deal of energy by harnessing the power of controlled nuclear reactions. Accidents at these plants are very rare, but they do happen.

The accident at the Chernobyl nuclear power plant in Ukraine (then part of the **USSR**), in April 1986, was probably the worst nuclear accident in history. The accident was mainly caused by the **reactor** being badly designed – but it raised serious concerns about the safety of the nuclear power industry, all around the world.

During a test, an explosion of steam destroyed the lid of a nuclear reactor and blew a hole in the roof of this building. This caused a fire and the smoke from the fire carried radioactivity far and wide.

The government kept the disaster a secret at first – but secrets tend to get out. The following day, workers at a nuclear power plant in Sweden found radioactive particles on their clothes. They checked their plant for leaks and eventually realised that the particles must have come in on the wind, from the USSR.

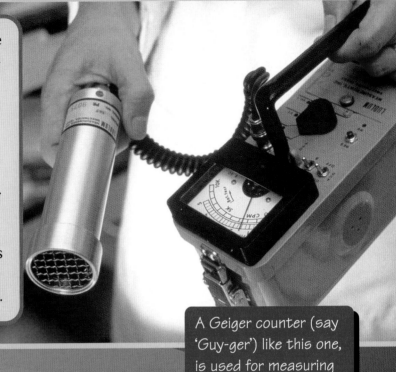

A Geiger counter (say 'Guy-ger') like this one, is used for measuring radioactivity.

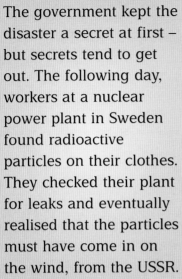

Thirty-one people died as a direct result of the accident, and many more have suffered with cancer. Everyone who lived within 30 kilometres of the plant was **evacuated** – over 100,000 people in all. The land is still dangerously radioactive, but already about 800 people – mostly older people – have moved back into the area, ignoring a government ban.

BANG!

Christmas crackers 'snap' because there is a tiny explosion between the ends of the two halves of the cracker's tape.

Do you know why party poppers bang? The smoke in the air and the smell of it should tell you that the bang is made by a small gunpowder explosion. When you pull the string, it sets off a small explosive charge which blows the top off the popper and pushes the streamers out. This is why the streamers come out so fast – and why you must never set one off aiming directly at someone's face.

There are many other things that explode which there isn't room to include in this book. Can you think of any more?

GLOSSARY

atom – the smallest part of any substance that can be identified as being that substance

Aztecs – a native people who ruled Mexico before the Spanish arrived in the 1500s

dormant – not active (the word really means 'sleeping')

evacuated – made to leave for safety reasons

fuse – the tube or string that sticks out of a firework or explosive and which is used to set it off

gravity – the force that makes things fall to the ground and keeps us standing on the Earth instead of floating away into space

Gunpowder Plot – A group of plotters, including Guy Fawkes, who planned to blow up the English king and parliament on 5 November 1605. They were caught and executed

Judas – according to the Bible, one of Jesus' followers who gave Jesus up to the Jewish authorities

kernel – an individual seed of corn

Marco Polo – an explorer from Venice who visited China in the 1200s

molten rock – rock beneath the Earth's surface that is so hot it becomes a liquid known as magma

radioactivity – powerful and dangerous rays given off by a nuclear reaction

reactor – the equipment or chamber inside a nuclear power station where the nuclear reactions actually take place

USSR – the Union of Soviet Socialist Republics, the name for Russia and some other countries it controlled until the late 1900s

INDEX

ash   24–25

atom   26

Aztecs   21

bamboo   6

Catherine wheel   8

Chernobyl   28–29

China   6, 11

Christmas crackers   4, 30

demolition   16–17, 18–19

eruption   22–23, 24–25

fireworks   4, 6–7, 8–9, 10–11, 12–13, 14

fireworks code   14

fuse   7, 12, 18

gas, gases   5, 6–7, 15, 24

gas leak   15

gravity   19

Great Fire of London   16

gunpowder   6–7, 8, 11, 30

Hiroshima   27

implosion   18–19

kernel   20–21

magma   22–23

molten rock   22–23

Mount St Helens   24–25

Nagasaki   27

Native Americans   21

New Year   10–11

nuclear   4–5, 26–27, 28–29

nuclear bomb   4, 5, 27

nuclear reaction   26–27, 28

popcorn   4, 20–21

pressure   4–5, 21, 23

radioactivity   5, 27, 28–29

rockets   6–7

San Francisco   17

Second World War   17

sparkler   6–7, 8

steam   5, 21, 28

volcanoes   4, 22–23, 24–25